Artistic Expressions of Transgender Youth

By Tony Ferraiolo, CPC

Camille
You Rock !!

Copyright

First published in the United States of America in
2015 by Tony Ferraiolo.

Edited by Jenn T. Grace & Niki Garcia.

Page layout by Maura Gianakos

Cover design by Matthew Upton

First edition, November 2015.

ISBN# 978-0-9966430-0-9

Library of Congress Catalog Card Number
2015914718

Dedication

This book is dedicated to all the transgender and
gender non-conforming youth who are in a state of struggle.
Stay strong…sending Love & Light

Acknowledgements

There have been so many people that have supported me and the creation of this book, that it would take a whole other book to name them all — here are just a few.

To my twin brother Nick Ferraiolo, you have been by my side since before we took our first breath. I can't thank you enough for all the love, support and laughs you bring into my life — you are always there when I need it the most.

Dru Levasseur, how do I begin to thank you? Your encouragement through this first book kept me believing that I could actually write it. You're my BFF and bring so much to my life. You, my friend, have helped me become who I am today, I can't thank you enough. Here's to our bromance…bbrrrtttt.

To my family…Mom, Dad, Frank, Felix, Sue, Claudia, Jennifer, Stephanie, Matthew and Angelina, thank you for being a part of this amazing journey. I know this journey hasn't always been the easiest for you, but you've shown time and again, love always prevails.

To my Manager Jenn T. Grace...WOW where do I start? You are my rock. I can't say thank you enough for your support with this book. It is a great feeling, knowing I am safe because you have my back. (BAV)

To the members of Translation, TransPACT, and Create Yourself, thank you for allowing me to be a part of your individual journeys.

Jay Loundes, you have brought so much joy into my life. You are like a son to me and I can't wait to witness the journey that lies in front of you.

A special shout out to Melissa Spears, Sally Tamarkin, Gretchen Raffa, and True Colors for all their support.

To the artists in this book: Avery K., Aubri, April, Rain, David, Edgar, Parker, Avery, Zane, Dave, Xander, Violet, Julissa, Kelly, Haley, Jonah, Jay, Van, Max, Samson, Sam, Sebastian, Spencer, and Erik. Thank you for allowing me to be your voice. You are all so amazingly courageous!

On Trans Kids and Their Art

Foreword by Andrew Solomon

The injunction to be oneself, put forward for adults in the 1960s, caught on for children in the free-to-be 1970s. But that language of liberal acceptance had boundaries. Little girls were encouraged to figure out how to enter the workforce and achieve personal fulfillment there. Little boys were allowed to like art. But sexual orientation was not up for discussion, and gender identity was not even on the collective radar. As gay and trans rights were established for adults, some attention went to the manifestations of such exceptional identities in children — but those attentions were mostly focused on "curing" the minds of those who were "diseased."

Today, we have recognized that to be transgender is to have an identity rather than an illness — an identity that can be extremely valuable to those who share it. We have begun to see that trans lives matter, that they are part of the spectrum of human diversity, and that many trans people celebrate their experience. We have understood that in most instances, trans is not something you become, but something you are, and that it often manifests in earliest childhood. Babies who can barely talk sometimes tell their parents on the changing table, "But I'm a boy!" or "But I'm a girl!" They learn in infancy that their gender is discordant with their natal anatomy. Their deepest knowledge of themselves is dismissed as idle fantasy.

In our enlightened time, we hear a great deal from trans adults, a good deal from doctors who work with the trans population, and a bit from the parents of trans kids.

But until now, we've heard relatively little from trans children themselves. Their voices are amplified in this collection and their experience is made clear. Some of the pain of such contradictory lives comes through, but so does some of the joy. These are stories of confusion, but also of surprising clarity. They reference loss, but also knowledge. They are deadly serious and also sometimes hilarious. The only successful model for parenting trans kids is attention to them, and this book is a sort of manual for such engagement. These children have laid bare the most inarticulate part of themselves. This is not about policy; this is about their inner reality. Tony Ferraiolo has led by example, insisting on the integrity of his identity and refusing the seductions of euphemism. He is what it means to be proud. But he took a rough road getting to psychic health, and that makes him a perfect match with children who are struggling to hatch a trans self.

For too long, being trans required universal furtiveness; people hid their own body history because it seemed a mark of shame. In this time of greater openness, people are free to choose, and may be stealth or out or may go back and forth depending on context. Words can be difficult for all children and are hardest for children whose very self resists common vocabulary. In drawings, these children achieve some freedom to express emotional truths for which they could not find words. Their drawings are childish in style but mature in their content. Trans kids have to grow up fast — not only because their focus on gender is often construed as a focus on sexuality, but also because their minds have to countenance the contradictory nature of human experience early and powerfully. In a time when art therapy has become a commonplace, these drawings look like the products of a workshop on healing. But though drawing them must have helped the artists, they are sure to be more help to those who encounter them here.

Preface

In 2008, after creating a support group for transgender teens, I began receiving phone calls and emails asking if I could create a support group for transgender children, ages 4–12. I knew these young children wouldn't benefit from a support group in the way that the teenagers did, but I did know they needed a special space where they could be themselves and express who they are in a supportive environment.

As an artist, my immediate thought was to start an art group; a place where transgender children can be themselves and dress in the clothes that they feel most comfortable in. I knew they would benefit from this environment, even if they were only able to be their full selves for an hour every three weeks.

I wanted to provide them with an outlet to creatively express their emotions. An outlet I wish I had when I was young, so when puberty came around they would create art and not turn to self-harm, like so many transgender youth do, myself included. My wish for them, and all transgender children, is to create — don't cut.

Before starting the first group I wrote down a few guidelines — the first and most important was to not bring up the topic of their gender. I wanted the children to be around each other, feel safe in the comfort that their peers are also going through the same struggles and understand them, and allow them for one hour to just be who they are, children.

In being honest with you I was very nervous at the first group. I had three kids show up ranging from 5-7 years old. One of the kids looked very anxious walking into group with a backpack and proceeded to the bathroom with their mother. They were changing into their "girl clothes." Upon doing so you could see a great big smile and a sense of relief while playing with Play-Doh for an hour. I vividly remember sitting back and listening to these children bond with one another, in a way I was sure they hadn't yet experienced with other friends of theirs.

There were two children in that first group that identified as female. They were comparing their shoes and barrettes. Based on the excitement in their voices, I could tell that this was most likely the first time they'd ever had this type of conversation with anyone. I overheard statements such as "Oh, I love your skirt, I have one just like it but it's pink not purple." In that first hour, with those three kids, I knew without a doubt that this art group would make a difference in their lives, and mine.

About two months into the group we were planning to make holiday cards together, when one of the children appeared very sad. When I asked everyone how they were doing, the one child said, "I'm really sad today." I asked if they wanted to share why. Their answer was, "I always feel sad when I can't be who I know I am."

I looked around the room and asked if anyone else had ever felt like that. Every one of them (including me) raised their hand. In that moment I passed them a piece of paper, originally meant for a holiday card, and asked them to draw what makes them sad. Then I asked if they could tell me exactly what the picture meant by writing on the back of it. For those too young to write, I wrote it for them. We continued to do this exercise anytime someone shared with the group their emotions. Realizing how incredibly powerful and healing this was I offered this to the teen support group as well. I automatically felt that the drawings and statements from these children and teens would be a great tool to educate those who are searching for a way to better understand the lives and emotions of transgender children.

I receive many calls from mental health providers and/or parents and the first thing they say to me is "I have a child that has gender identity issues." My response is usually something to the effect of "No, they don't have gender identity issues, it's everyone around them that has an issue with their gender identity." Everyone has a gender identity, but yet it is only toward the transgender community that people think to ask the question, "Are you sure?" or "How can they know that? They are way too young." I can assure you these children, just like myself, know their gender identity.

What Makes This Book Different?

There are plenty of books in existence about transgender youth. There are a lot of good people, trying to give good information, and for the most part they are. But you might be asking yourself what makes this book different than the others. This book is different because you will be educated directly by transgender children and teens. Not by a medical professional. Not by a life coach. Not even by me. This book will illustrate how transgender children and teens feel and think about themselves, as told through their art. Each drawing is accompanied by a statement where each child describes what their art means to them.

My wish for you is to walk away with from this book series with a better understanding of what transgender youth are going through. I want you to see and understand that their struggles are real and need to be acknowledged. I personally know how it feels when you know who you are, but people around you are saying, "No, you're not, that's not who you are." We can't do this to another transgender child. Too many young lives are lost because these children are not able to express themselves. They are not coming out transgender for attention, to hurt anyone, to embarrass their families — they are coming out because they can't hold it in any longer and it is who they are.

Quite often I hear people say "These kids have it easy, they have a lot of resources these days." Sure, there are a lot more resources out there today than when I was transitioning. However, the internal struggle never changes despite the amount of resources available. It's not easy for a kid to say, "I'm trans." They are often struggling to have their identities taken seriously by those around them. They often hear disheartening statements like, "How can you know this? You're too young." or "Sure! Today you are transgender, what will you be tomorrow? This is just a phase."

Transgender children are acutely aware of what they can lose by uttering those three words, "I am trans." They've seen kids be thrown out of their houses for being transgender, they've witnessed parents shutting them out because of their gender identity and they know that transgender people are targets of violence every single day in this world, simply because they are transgender. Yet, they still have the courage to say, "This is who I am." We must acknowledge that, there is no alternative.

My dream is to live in a world where we see every transgender child consider being transgender like I consider being Italian. You know what I mean? I know I am Italian, it's somewhere in the back of my brain, but it does not define me. It is one piece of who I am. We must allow transgender children to simply be who they are.

What Does Body Dysphoria Feel Like?

In my estimation, I would guess that close to 90% of the transgender children and teens I have worked with struggle with some degree of body dysphoria. Since I started this work, and through my own personal struggles with body dysphoria, I have always viewed this as the most damaging aspect to my community. There is a big misunderstanding about transgender people and their bodies and that lack of knowledge creates a large gap between medical staff, mental health providers, parents and their transgender patient or child. This leads all parties involved sometimes at a loss for words when their patient or child is expressing that they are uncomfortable in the body they were born in.

In late 2013, I began coaching a 13-year-old transgender male. He was in such distress that he was cutting himself and then stitching it back up. During one of our coaching sessions, he started crying. With his face in his hands he screamed, "You don't get it! I was born in the wrong body! I am trapped in this body!" I was at a loss for words.

Even though I felt the same way for years, I didn't know how to make it better for him. A few days later, it came to me. I realized his depression and anxiety were coming directly from his body dysphoria. I thought, wow, how would anyone feel if they thought they were born wrong or trapped in the wrong body? The feeling of being wrong can cause depression and the thought of being trapped can cause anxiety. From that moment on, whenever a youth expressed that they were born in the wrong body or trapped in the wrong body, I would gently correct them by saying that they were born in their body and if they needed to change their body, we're going to help them through it and most importantly, I told them they were not alone.

I am happy to report that my client's distress was greatly minimized. I would love to say it was nonexistent, but we've only won half of the battle. Next was coaching him on how to move forward in his transition without the medical treatment he so desperately needed. What worked for this client, this transgender teenager, was helping him shift his thoughts of "This will never happen" to "Just because it's not going to happen today, doesn't mean it won't happen someday." As I learned through my coaching program at the Institute for Professional Excellence in Coaching (iPEC), you first change the thought, then the emotion changes and then the action changes.

Artistic Expressions Of Transgender Youth

I asked over 100 kids to answer the following questions.

- What does body dysphoria feel like?

- If you had all the money in the world, what would be the first thing you would buy?

This book contains 24 of the most moving responses.

What Does Body Dysphoria Feel Like?

Avery

Age 16

I'm ripping at my flesh trying to tear away my femininity.

GO AWAY!!!!

Aubri

Age 14

What gender dysphoria (and body) is, is the constant want to almost explode, to burst free from being locked in a body and hurting. And what makes it worse is the oppressing media stereotypes of women. So I feel like I have to live up to [those stereotypes]. In my case, I am the girl trapped in a male body.

Aubri 14

19

April

Age 15

I can't see what I want to see.

NO ARMOR

I can't see what
I wan't to see...

Kills Me
Every
Time

April, 15

21

Rain

Age 16

Body dysphoria is like….

- Not recognizing yourself in mirrors.

- Not having control over your body.

- Feeling like you're presenting yourself to the world all wrong.

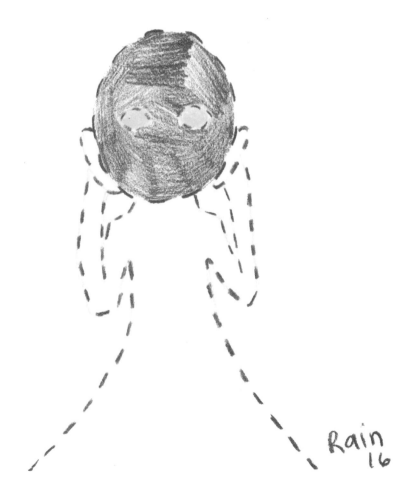

Rain
16

23

David

Age 15

Being branded on your forehead something that will forever discriminate you.

David 15

25

Edgar

Age 14

Body dysphoria to me feels like being locked in a cage (as cliché as that sounds). Sometimes I feel superior, but my "human form" is keeping me down. There are lots of things I'll never be able to experience because of my body. Even worse, many people think that my aforementioned human form has to define me. I drew weapons around my cage because I feel like I am being tortured for having any confidence, and my body is my punishment.

Edgar age 14

Parker

Age 16

I feel as if I am in constant hell. I feel paranoid that each and every person views me as a female and that causes constant anxiety. I live in constant fear of someone calling me a girl, and when someone does, I can't feel my body.

Parker 16

Avery

Age 17

It's total disconnect and pain and misery. Total chaos in my mind. Makes me want to do anything to escape the hell and torture I'm in.

31

Zane

Age 15

What dysphoria looks like to me is pain and static where comfort and identity should be.

Zane 15

Dave

Age 16

Not matching mental body parts to physical...I actually renamed my anatomy to FIT what it SHOULD BE.

Alexander

Age 16

For me dysphoria comes from the words I hear, from others and from my own mind. Sometimes it seems like the only way to get away from a huge monster on my back is self-harm.

37

Violet

Age 17

You can't move. You just sit there in the corner and watch everyone walk by, and you can't move.

Violet
17 ³/₄

Julissa

Age 17

It's the feeling of dying inside, when all I want to do is live a happy life.

Julissa, 17

41

Kelly

Age 21

Dysphoria is when your body is a prison that you'll never escape. It's when the body and society betray the soul. It's kind of a buzz kill.

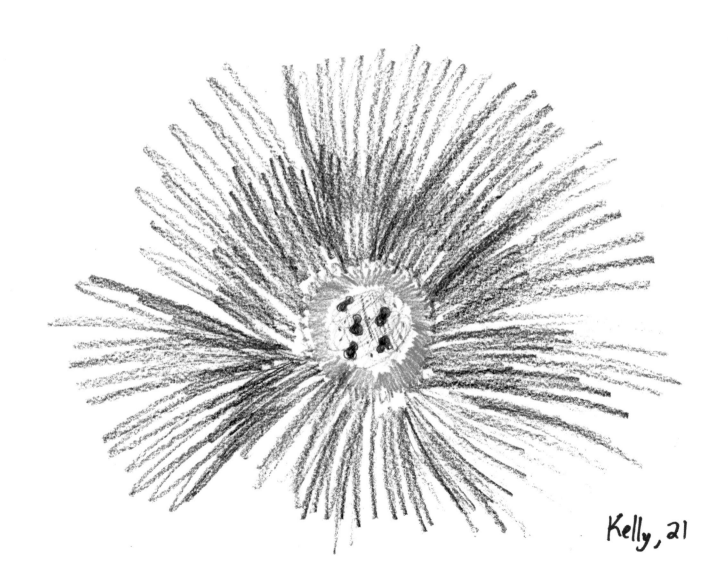

Kelly, 21

43

If You Had All The Money In The World,
What Would Be The First Thing You Would Buy?

The next question I began asking the children in my art group was, "If you had all the money in the world, what would be the first thing you would buy?" In asking this question I was hoping to learn a few things, such as;

1. What percentage of transgender youth are in need of some kind of medical intervention? If they are, how much distress is it causing them?

2. For those transgender youth that experience discomfort with their bodies, what age does it start?

I wasn't surprised by the percentage of drawings that had something to do with some type of surgery and/or other medical intervention. It is so important to provide transgender youth with a clear vision that their lives won't be filled with pain and sadness. They, like any other child who is not transgender, need to see that they have a future. A future where they have support from their parents, their schools and their health providers. They need to know that if they are struggling with body dysphoria, that they will be provided the care to minimize the emotional stresses that come along with it. They need to know that they won't be judged or shamed into conforming to a person they are not. As soon as they are allowed to be their authentic selves they will shift to a place of less anxiety and depression.

Depression and anxiety are often discussed in the teen group that I facilitate. In my experience, most transgender teens are more focused on taking care of everyone around them than taking care of themselves. In a lot of cases they will mask their depression and anxiety with a smile and by telling everyone that they are okay. I feel this false sense of being okay happens when they are fearful of disappointing their support system or when they are fearful that if they admit to their depression and/or anxiety they will be looked at as having a mental disorder. The stigma of a mental disorder has deeper, damaging effects for transgender youth because it is often blamed as the root of what is "making" them transgender. I cannot emphasize this enough, we cannot judge or shame transgender youth to the point where they are too afraid to talk about their depression.

When a group member shares with us that they are struggling with their depression, it is accompanied by a lot of emotion. They start crying uncontrollably, because they've been holding it in for so long. When this does happen, I look to see the reactions of the other teens. Most of them have tears in their eyes, because they have felt or are feeling the same way. Others will simply put their heads down, because it is too hard to deal with in that moment.

This is why asking them the question, "If you had all the money in the world, what be the first thing you would buy?" was so important. Their drawings and descriptions gave them an outlet to open up about what they needed. Not every transgender child would buy a medical procedure, but you will see several drawings in this section associated with gender affirming surgeries and see the phrases "All better" or "My freedom!" in relation to those surgeries.

If You Had All The Money In The World,
What Would Be The First Thing You Would Buy?

Haley

Age 6

I would buy a mermaid right away!

Jonah

Age 6

I am gender non-conforming and I would buy myself a very colorful dress!!

Jay

Age 8

I'd buy a mansion!

Amansion   Jay 8

Van

Age 17

Have my own kids show & colonize space

Have my own Kid's Show & Colonize Space

Van, 17

Max

Age 17

I would buy my freedom...my chest!

Samson

Age 18

I would buy my chest surgery and since I have all the money in the world, I would buy my best friend his chest surgery too.

Sam

Age 18

Every makeup, shoe and accessory store and mall!!

Sam, 18

Sebastian

Age 17

Security for life! I'm always so terrified that I won't make it through life without starving on the street.

Sebastian

17

Spencer

Age 20

A really cool pick-up truck

Spencer, 20

Erik

Age 19

"No comment needed"

ERIK-19

67

About The Author

When I realized I was transgender, I didn't do cartwheels. I didn't know anyone else like me. I remember going to the beach and crying, wondering if I wanted to live. Wondering, if my life was so unbearable now, how would it be if I came out as transgender? Then something happened. I realized that I had the opportunity to create myself into the person who I always wanted to be. I remember asking myself, what do I need to do to become that person? There was a very long list of "To Do's." I knew that the anger I carried would transfer over into the person I wanted to create, so I worked very hard to let go of it. I forgave everyone who abused me, including myself. Once I let go of my anger, my soul filled with compassion. I believe that you must see the dark before you see the light — and that some of us must struggle through the challenges we face because it is part of the growth. I can honestly say that I would not change anything about my past. I truly believe that my past is what created "Tony."

See The Film

Tony's life work has been featured in the award winning documentary *A Self-Made Man* by filmmaker Lori Petchers. To see when and where the film is airing please visit: http://aselfmademanfilm.com/

a film by Lori Petchers

a
Self-Made
Man

5E FILMS PRESENTS "A SELF-MADE MAN" FEATURING TONY FERRAIOLO
SCORE BY DINA GUTTMANN MUSIC BY BRYAN SENTI
PRODUCED, DIRECTED, & FILMED BY LORI PETCHERS

"I will not forget who I was, I honor her. Because she had the strength to say no to the suicide, to be strong enough to survive all this and allow me to be Tony."

Hire Tony

Speaking

Tony began his professional speaking career in 2005. He is known for infusing his stories of the struggles of his gender transition with insight and humor. He is committed to delivering engaging, thought-provoking, and heart-felt messages that will leave the audience with a greater awareness of their own life potential and the motivation to start living the life they always imagined.

Training

Tony has trained in a variety of professional settings since 2009. He is known for his humor and ability to make light of a sometimes-challenging situation. His trainings leave the audience with a new found perspective on what it is like to be transgender and how that newly acquired knowledge can help them better understand and support their patients, staff, co-workers, students, and children. His commitment to delivering a thought-provoking and heart felt training will leave you wanting more and beginning to realize your true potential to start living the life you've always imagined.

If you'd like to book Tony for speaking or training, please visit *www.tonyferraiolo.com*